Setting the House in Order

Building According to Pattern

Stan E. DeKoven, Ph.D.

Setting the House in Order

Building According to Pattern

Stan E. DeKoven, Ph.D.

ISBN: 978-1-931178-02-0

Copyright © 2008 Stan E. DeKoven

Revised and Expanded 2024

Vision Publishing
P.O. Box 1680
530 11th Street
Ramona, CA 92065
www.booksbyvision.org

All rights in this book are reserved. No part of this book may be reproduced in any manner whatsoever without the written permission of the author except brief quotations embodied in critical articles or reviews.

Acknowledgements

This book is based upon a series of messages preached at Fontana Christian Fellowship International Ministries in Fontana, CA, (now called Frequency). This dynamic fellowship, lead by Pastors Gary and Gina Holley, honor me by allowing me to conduct an annual series of four messages for their congregation. My gift to them, and subsequently their gift to the body of Christ is the production of this annual book. Thanks again Gary and Gina for your faithfulness, love, and honor, and may the Lord continue to bless the congregation as they come into greater alignment with God's patterns.

Further, this book is a result of many years of observation of Christ's glorious church, as seen in the world today. Many of the thoughts that formed the writing were shaped by significant relationships I will always cherish. These include, but are not limited to my first Pastor, Rev. Lee Speakman, a man of true piety, Dr. Joseph Bohac, a pioneering pastor of imminence though often unappreciated gifting, Dr. Ken Chant a theologian extraordinaire, friend and co-laborer for Christ and Dr. Apostle George Runyan, my partner in Kingdom building in our region and beyond.

I must further acknowledge the many wonderful churches I am honored to work with, and their dedicated leaders. To a person, they are doing all they can to lead congregations, conducting some of the hardest work on the planet, with little hope and glory or financial reward. They are the real warriors, and I am enriched by their integrity in struggle.

Finally, I must thank the dedicated and patient staff of Vision International University. When I write I am not terribly good at my primary duties, and my faithful co-laborers help keep the ship afloat. My thanks to Maureen Kelley, Dr. Delores Horsman, Drs Tal, and Dee Klaus (thanks for helping as a manuscript reader), Pastor Mark McElwee, my wonderful daughter Rebecca DeKoven. You all do so much with so little.

Foreword

There is a cry in the church that goes out from both its leaders and people. What is the house of God supposed to look like? And how is it to function? We are angry, discouraged, frustrated, depressed, disappointed, abused; and simply put, tired of most of the structure we've seen in the local church ministry today. Our current framework is failing more rapidly than it's succeeding. Operating churches are closing at a faster rate than new churches are being opened.

Dr. Stan DeKoven has taken the dare to rediscover what God's Word outlines for the local church and its "biblical structure and design." If the success of our churches were to be based on a "program" or a "prodigy," they would not be encountering the enormous breakdowns morally, spiritually, physically, and financially that they are experiencing today. We believe that God understands the DNA of the church far better than man does. Rediscovering the apostolic and prophetic fundamental roles and their groundbreaking principles for church structure is no longer an option, but a demand! Read and be challenged by God's order for the church today.

Pastors Gary and Gina Holley

Frequency Church, Fontana, CA

Table of Contents

Acknowledgements 3

Foreword 5

Table of Contents 7

Introduction to Second Edition 9

Chapter 1: The Church Observed 17

Chapter 2: Four Types of Churches 31

Chapter 3: Missing Elements of Church Life 39

Chapter 4: The Heart of a King 63

Chapter 5: The Characteristics of the House 81

Conclusion 91

Other Books by the Author 93

Introduction to Second Edition

It has been 10+ years since I wrote this booklet. The writing began as musings or church life, was expanded into a sermon series, and eventually written out. These thoughts on the life of the church have gone around the world chiefly through our Vision International Network.

One might ask, has that much changed in the last 10 years? Well, both in the church and around the world, change has been rapid. Social media, which is often antisocial and poor media, is the premier form of communication. Cultural trends especially in the Western Church has moved the theological and sociological needle in the direction of post-modern thought, often dumbing down the gospel of the Kingdom to powerless platitudes or politically incorrect invective. Being a bible believing Christian isn't as easy as it used to be, which requires response and adjustment, based upon biblical principles and patterns. In other words, some things have got to change!

Adding to the relative dysfunction and disruption of the modern church has been the devastation caused by a worldwide pandemic and wars (Ukraine and Israel). Of course, in spite of these serious and painful world problems millions continue to come to faith in Christ, and the Kingdom of God continues to advance.

A few weeks ago, I re-read Erwin Raphael McManis book, "The Barbarian Way" (Nelson Books 2005) and was struck by a couple of quotes related to church life

> "When it came down to it, they (the 1st Century Jew's) loved their civilized religion more then they longed to honor the God who created them. They would rather have the temple than the Presence." (page 11)

and referring to the church at large:

> "We have become believers rather than experiencers. To know God in the Scriptures always went beyond information to intimacy."

The church has always been a dynamic organization, that is fed by obedient adherence to Gods Word, inspired and empowered by the Holy Spirit. As such The Kingdom of God will always advance, regardless of what we might see, and Jesus Christ remains Lord and always will. Our task in the 21st Century is to work to see the Kingdom truly advance...Which is more than church growth (but includes that) and includes the transformation of nations for Christ glory.

We must remember that the church, the bride of Christ, the one new man in the earth, is God's vehicle for the transformation of our world.

So, in the second edition of my thoughts on the church, I will reinforce foundational Principles, expanding on some and minimizing others, and refresh what seems to be the essential components of setting the house of God in order again, for his glory.

Further Introduction

In a conference a few years ago, Pastor Terry Crist of Tulsa, Oklahoma at the time used the term "transitional leadership" in reference to the present status of the church. Pastor Crist' primary perspective presented was that the church is in a time of immense and important transition, where older leadership are passing, or having to release the baton of leadership to a younger generation. This younger generation, different than all previous ones, is sensing a change in church life. The emphasis on big meetings, big buildings and big finances is shifting towards networking for God's kingdom and coalition building on Apostolic and Prophetic lines. An acknowledgement has been made and gratitude shown to the great leaders of the past few decades. However, a new generation is emerging with a desire to return to authentic New Testament patterns of Christianity, centered on the teachings of Christ, the Apostles doctrine and prophetic vision and pronunciation. The Lord is setting his house in order. The order of the house; the materials to build with, the plans and purposes of God can be found in the written revelation of Christ. Paul stated to the church at Ephesus that the church is to be founded on the Apostles and Prophets (Eph. 2:20), Christ himself being the corner of the building. Most churches in the 21st century have been built on pastoral ministry or by teachers and evangelists in the office of a pastor. Again, we should always be grateful for every conversion to Christ and churches being planted, by whatever means. Pastoral ministry, as with all 5-fold gifts to the church are vital for spiritual maturity (Eph. 4:11-16). However, foundations are to be built by the gifts fundamental to the process, as the foundation is built by two ascension gifts (Ephesians 2:20) to be briefly discussed here.

The Apostle

Many debate the legitimacy of modern-day apostolic ministry. Rather than debate, the viewpoint of this book, is that this gift is active and essential for the next (final?) move of God. The bible discusses various characteristics of a true apostle (sent one), which includes going, preaching with signs and wonders following, and church planting and strengthening. Added to this and of importance to this study is the governmental aspect to this gift. That is, as demonstrated in the ministry of James and Paul, one primary aspect of their call was the organization and establishment of godly rule for the church of the locality. Historically, this function has been relegated to Bishops, presbyters, trustees, directors, elders, and deacons. However, as important as all these offices are, they must be subordinate to a called, anointed, and sent (not self-proclaimed) apostle, especially when working in their sphere of influence and in tandem with a true prophet of God. It is Paul the apostle who, in Ephesus and through his many letters, sets the house in order for proper growth and functioning to occur in Christ's body, as Paul did in Antioch under the initial authority of Barnabas. (A simple look at 1 and 2 Corinthians), gives us clarity. Here Paul addresses a very dicey church leadership situation, one not far from some of the issues we have to confront today. Paul confronts the leadership in the city, rebuking them for not taking appropriate action. They respond well, bring discipline, but essentially miss the point of the discipline, which was to produce repentance but didn't require restoration (which finally did occur). Paul as no doubt did refer and other apostles had the authority and responsibility to bring correction to the churches they had relationships with. This aspect of apostles ministry is certainly needed today.

The Prophet

Further and equally foundational in building God's Kingdom, both trans-local and local, is the ministry of the prophet. The prophet in proper office is able to speak the mind of Christ, the vision for the house, into the local corporate body of believers. As it were, the prophet is gifted to hear from heaven and give direction and purpose for the church, speaking life and power into the church. Thus, the mandate and specific intent for the church is provided by the Holy Spirit through the prophetic utterance, which will always align itself with God's word. Though the prophet may speak personally to individuals within a congregation, this is neither the primary function nor the most necessary component of the gift of prophecy. He/she is to speak as an oracle of God for the edification of the saints and to set in motion the divine purposes of God for a region.

Without these foundational gifts working in tandem, churches by and large are built incomplete and weak. In Proverbs it states that "If the foundations be destroyed what can even the righteous do?" Well, the righteous have been functioning to the best of their ability on a weakened or incomplete foundation, without prophetic insight into their divine destiny. The new orders of leaders with an understanding of the foundational offices will by God's grace and in his mercy "re-build the age-old foundations and restore the breach" (Isaiah 58:12).

The intent of this manuscript is to provide a thoroughly biblical view, using typological application of scripture, a picture of the church God desires. The Old Testament and New Testament words used for a building or house provide a fresh illumination of God's purposes for his church. Beginning with the foundation and moving to the highest place, the components of a whole house will be described and illustrated. Further, principles are presented rather than specific plans or blueprints being provided for the architectural and operational plans for God's building ...his church, which is the instrument for the establishment of his kingdom reign in the earth. "By wisdom a house is built and by understanding it is established; and by knowledge the rooms are filled with all precious and pleasant gifts." (Proverbs 24: 3-4) No specific type of government fits all situations, but principles and patterns found in scripture are essential to build a healthy house.

And...We need ALL 5

Of course, a proper foundation is essential, but does not make for a complete house. Building out the house makes a home possible. Thus, we need all five ascension gifts, apostles, prophets, Evangelists, Pastors, Teachers, plus Elders, Deacons and various ministries all serving and deferring to one another. For the sake of brevity and to remain on point I won't describe each area of ministry (Service), or the gifting needed, but simply to note we all need each other, unified with apostolic/prophetic Kingdom ministry.

"Church isn't where you meet. Church isn't a building. Church is what you do. Church is who you are. Church is the human outworking of the person of Jesus Christ. Let's not go to Church, let's be the Church"

Bridget Willard

Chapter 1: The Church Observed

It has been said that great preaching alone will not build the church. For that matter, neither will great prayer, fasting, spiritual warfare or Madison Avenue strategies. Great churches, as measured by God's standards, are ones who fulfill the purpose of the Father by building according to Biblical pattern.

The Apostle Peter, in describing the church of Jesus Christ stated, "…you also, as living stones, are being built up as a spiritual house for a holy priesthood to offer up spiritual sacrifices acceptable to God though Jesus Christ."

The Father's intention has always been to have a house for His presence, a spiritual house. The earthly expression of this is the church. The church, the "ecclesia," the entity Christ promised to build began on the day of Pentecost, a dynamic, living organism. Sadly, what is often called the church, made up of Kingdom citizens gathered together, infecting all segments of the city or locality, is far less than the dynamic living stones of royal priests described by Peter. Our only assumption from this reality is that something has gone terribly wrong. After nearly 2000 years of church life, one wonders what has happened with the church.

Perhaps a brief commentary will help. Some partially dated, but still relevant statistics (Barna, 2012) indicate that the church in Western nations is highly marginalized (not really considered important in public debate). Christian marriages ending in divorce occur at a similar or higher rate to non-believers; in spite of the statistics touted on Christian T.V., church attendance has descended, where the "NONES" are outpacing attendees, bible reading is at a minimum, biblical illiteracy at an all-time high. Predictions of a worldwide revival, or an escape from it all surface periodically, but the revival seems to fizzle and the rapture…well, we still hope. What is happening? Why is the church, which started so triumphantly, experiencing such inconsistency or lethargy?[1] A good question which I will attempt to answer moving forward.

Of course, the church remains God's principal instrument for national transformation, and the preaching of the cross remains the only way to salvation. And, we must acknowledge the church has always had problems.

Paul, Peter, and the Foundation

When it comes to putting the house of God in order, there is no one more authoritative than Paul and Peter. As previously stated, the foundation of the church was laid by the Apostles and Prophets (Eph. 2:20) and is discussed by both Paul and Peter as they labored to ensure that the churches that they oversaw were strong, with healthy, kingdom focused leaders. I have purposely chosen Paul to speak first as it were from the church that caused him the greatest joy and trouble, the church in Corinth.

---

[1] It must be noted that it is primarily the Western church, which is in a holding pattern, or in decline: In two thirds world churches, the Kingdom continues to grow., most notably China, which is experiencing great growth, and is doing so with limited help or influence from the West.

In 1 Corinthians 3:1-14 we read (you were briefly introduced in the introduction):

> "And I, brethren, could not speak to you as to spiritual men, but as to men of flesh, as to babes in Christ. I gave you milk to drink, not solid food; for you were not yet able to receive it; even now you are not yet able. For you are still fleshly. For since there is jealousy and strife among you, are you not fleshly, and are you not walking like mere men? For when one says, I am of Paul; and another, I am of Apollos; are you not mere men? What then is Apollos? And what is Paul? Servants through whom you believed, even as the Lord gave opportunity to each? I planted, Apollos watered, but God was causing the growth. So then neither the one who plants, nor the one who waters is anything, but God who causes the growth. Now he who plants, and he who waters are one, and each will receive his own reward according to his own labor. For we are God's fellow-workers; you are God's field, God's building.
>
> According to the grace of God, which was given to me, as a wise master builder, I laid a foundation, and another is building upon it. But let each man be careful how he builds upon it. For no man can lay a foundation other than the one which is laid, which is Jesus Christ. Now if any man builds upon this foundation gold, silver, precious stones, wood, hay, straw, each man's work will become evident; for the day will show it, because it is to be revealed by fire; and the fire itself will test the quality of each

man's work. If any man's work which he has built upon it remains, he shall receive a reward."

Because of the problems in this highly charismatic church, Paul was compelled to withhold the greater revelation of God's purpose for the churches good. The reason for this, as presented by Paul was due to some specific problems indicating wrong priorities for the church in Corinth. Essentially, the church was highly immature and most likely insecure, with wrong priorities or areas of sin including...

Worldliness, which is to have the wrong values towards life. Rather than having a dependence on God, they were looking to man (in this case, good men) but did so from a wrong motivation. Everyone has a worldview which directs their life purposes. For the Corinthians, and like most people regardless of culture, they sought to raise their status or esteem by identifying with their favorite preacher. Rather than recognizing that the Lord can work through anyone willing to yield their lives to the Lord, they looked to have their special, personal preacher to speak their favorite doctrine. Sadly, this selectivity or favoritism demonstrated an immaturity, a desire to please man rather than to please the Lord. This is a major problem in the church today as well. Of course, this is not just seen with preachers (local or media stars) but worship leaders, style of music, comfort of chairs, etc. Further, they were filled with...

Jealousy, amounting to covetousness, rooted in fear. All jealousy is rooted in a fear, generally a fear that someone else will have more, receive greater blessings, happier times than the jealous one. The Bible states that fear has torment (1 Jn 4:18), not a good thing. That is, fear is often the opposite of love; the love of God, which is to be shown abroad in our hearts, filling us with thanksgiving regardless of who is being blessed or who prospers, is what we are to aiming for. We are challenged by Jesus to go beyond the love of the righteous. Pharisee (love God; love your neighbor) but to love like Jesus loves, perfectly, compassionately, with grace and truth.

Apparently, the people were also **quarrelling** about who the best preacher was, and probably other issues in the life of the church (you can use your imagination). These quarrels, over who had the better and more powerful father figure, stemming from insecurity and immaturity, lead them to function in the ordinary, rather than from a supernatural orientation towards life.

Immorality…It is important to note that Paul was intolerant towards tolerance…especially tolerating sin that could hurt the body of Christ for which Christ died and on behalf he labored…It is doubtful if Paul would have been so strong in his opposition to the man in sin (sleeping with his father's wife, essentially the man's stepmother (uck!!) if he was a member of the congregation, but since he was apparently a leader, Paul was incensed. Again, not as much about the type of sin, but the leaderships in ability to address it. Problems happen…sin happens…healthy leaders must take responsibility and act.

Comparisons: Divide and Conquer

One aspect of human nature, especially empowered by the enemy of our souls, is to divide where weakness is found. This can be especially seen when parents are in disagreement, or when church members know that the leadership is not on the same page. When children believe there is opportunity to get between mom and dad, an irresistible force moves them to test to see if the parents are united and strong, or disunited and easily divided. It is not that they want the division, which leads to insecurity and acting out, but the opposite. Yet, like a sign that says wet paint, do not touch, the desire to test the strength of the parental dyad is irresistible. The analogy can be easily seen in church life, which is often a microcosm of the dysfunction of the families in the church.

However, the Kingdom is to be team oriented, and those laboring in the kingdom as God's servants deserve to be honored and respected. For leaders, especially those that labor in the word of God, deserve their wages, but the glory is God's. It is true that many present-day spiritual leaders are little more than circus performers and professional actors. That was not the case in Corinth; and it rarely is in local churches (again, I am focusing on the church, not Christian Television, a bit of an oxymoron). Whoever the preacher is, whatever the programs are, if the person leading is doing their best, according to the gift and grace given (Rom. 12:3-7), they deserve to be respected. Dishonoring through dividing and conquering is a major problem, which must be dealt with if we are going to see God's church brought to order.

We must all remember that God's house is his people; the building is secondary. Yet how much time is spent on the maintenance of buildings, rather than the ministry to people. In fact, as a family we are to labor together for the glory of God in our life and witness. There is no room for pettiness, quarrels, or division; but let me give one caution. Perfect will never come, offenses always do, but we must be willing to work through problems which are inevitable in relationships and must learn to be co-laborers together for the greater purposes of the Kingdom in our locality.

Paul's concern, as was Peter's, and should be for any leader with apostolic focus is to see God's house, made up of his people, not the building or the marquee, built for God's glory. To build the House of God effectively, a foundation must be laid. Thus, building the house of God is the purpose, therefore we must be careful how we build; his house is a place where God's spirit dwells, where his people gather, where the Word is preached and where family, true family is established.

Peters Perspective

1 Peter 2:4-10 reads;

> *"And coming to Him as to a living stone, rejected by men, but choice and precious in the sight of God, you also as living stones, are being built up as a spiritual house for a holy priesthood, to offer up spiritual sacrifices acceptable to God through Jesus Christ. For this is contained in Scripture: 'Behold I lay in Zion a choice stone, a precious corner stone, and he who believes in Him shall not be disappointed.' This precious value, then, is for you who believe, but for those who disbelieve, 'The stone which the builders rejected, this became the very corner stone.' And 'A stone of stumbling and a rock of offense,' for they stumble because they are disobedient to the word, and to this doom they were also appointed. But you are a Chosen Race, a Royal Priesthood, a Holy Nation, A people for God's own possession, that you may proclaim the excellencies of Him who has called you*

out of darkness into His marvelous light; for you once were not a people, but now you have received mercy."

As we discuss the setting of the house or community of saints in order, it is necessary to understand who we are in relationship to who Jesus is, for identity produces purpose. Jesus is the living stone, or a living foundation of the purposes of God, precious to the Father, and we are living stones, a part of the spiritual house of God. The scriptures teach us that we are a holy priesthood with the privilege of worshipping Almighty God. As holy priests to the Lord, we are a part of an ever-expanding Kingdom of God. Because we have received mercy from the Lord by our receiving Christ' grace and forgiveness, we are now a chosen people, the New Israel of God, (fulfilling not replacing Israel of old) a holy nation under the ownership of the Lord for his purposes.

Both Peter and Paul recognized early, probably through their own trials and troubles, that knowing who we are, and who we are not, in the Kingdom of God is a key to successful life in the Lord. In light of the very dysfunctional patterns, we often find in the local congregation, it is essential that we again review what the Lord expects of us, and what a truly functional church would look and function like.

The church in Corinth, as is well understood, was both dynamic (full expression of the gifts of the Holy Spirit) and significantly immature. It must be rightly assumed that the foundation for health and success was established through Paul's ministry. As a wise master builder, he insured that their start was fastened securely to Christ the Rock. However, they were full of divisions, filled with jealousy, had to be spoon fed to survive, and lacked sufficient understanding of their corporate responsibility to one another as the Temple of the Holy Spirit. Paul did not commend them, nor condone their immortality or lack of accountability. In fact, his letters were precisely written to do more than comment on their state of affairs, but to correct them, by distance if possible, in person if needed.

It is easy to look at the Corinthians with a smug self-righteousness, but sadly, conditions in the church, especially the Pentecostal/Charismatic wing of the church, has significant parallel to our brothers and sisters of antiquity. Some recent, some public, some not, situations, frequently seen in church life will illustrate the similarities.

A television preacher divorces his wife, marries another woman within days of the divorce, with no biblical grounds. When confronted about his behavior, he states that God had not called him to marriage, but to ministry. He continues pastoring his church and remains a popular T.V. personality.

Another minister, well known and loved, is caught in a form of horrible immortality. He apologizes, does not preach for three months (though continues to lead the church), and continues his ministry.

Many, many other examples could be sited, but the point is clear. There is a high degree of acceptance of men (women) of power using their prominence for pleasure and personal gain. This is expected in the world (i.e., former President Clinton a prime example, or President Trump), but it is never acceptable in the leadership of Christ' church.

Of course, these are not the only dysfunctions of the day. For years we (the church at large) have given too much credence to charisma over character, have focused too much on form (especially in worship, music, often trite or even unbiblical) rather than substance, have used techniques borrowed from suspect sources to gather more congregants, rather than raising disciples filled with life and power. We (the leaders) have encouraged an even wider clergy/laity split, where we sit on the platform, the pious, the professional, who perform the rituals of spiritual life while the passive part timers are only required to participate by sitting and giving (usually under compulsion). The priesthood of the believers seems lost; the purpose of the five-fold ministry (to equip for maturity and service) is often lost in our frantic search for more professionally produced programs.

In the midst of the difficulties easily observed, we must not assume that all is lost. Certainly not. In fact, we must assume that much of what God the Father desired for Christ' church is visible, viable, and victoriously fulfilling the mandate of the Great Commission. Cynicism must be avoided, yet we must not bury our head, pretending that (as my Australian friends might state) "she'll be right mate" and not address with serious thought, prayer, and discussion of the patterns of modern church life that appear contrary to God's word (and in many cases, simple common sense).

The Apostles Perspective

Most would concur that the Apostle Paul was/is the preeminent purveyor of what is intended by the Lord for his church. Paul's burden in prayer was that Christ would be formed in all men, and the church would be triumphant in its purpose. As in Corinth, already eluded too, Paul often had to clean up problems, sometimes done via print, sometimes in person. Certainly, we need apostolic voices and prophetic power to speak to the issues of our day, as Paul did to his. A brief review of Pauline perspective might help our thinking.

In Acts 20:17-27, Paul addresses the leadership of the dynamic church in Ephesus. He states,

> *"From Miletus he sent to Ephesus and called to him the elders of the church. And when they had come to him, he said to them, 'You yourselves know, from the first day that I set foot in Asia, how I was with you the whole time, serving the Lord with all humility and with tears and with trials which came upon me through the plots of the Jews; how I did not shrink from declaring to you anything that was profitable, and teaching you publicly and from house to house, solemnly testifying to both Jews and Greeks of repentance toward God and faith in our Lord Jesus Christ. And now, behold, bound by the Spirit, I am on my way to Jerusalem, not knowing what will happen to me there, except that the Holy Spirit solemnly testifies to me in every city, saying that bonds and afflictions await me. But I do not consider my life of any account as dear to myself, so that I may finish my course and the ministry which I received from the Lord Jesus, to testify solemnly of the gospel of the grace of God. And now, behold, I know that all of you, among whom I went about preaching the kingdom, will no longer see my face. Therefore, I testify to you this day that I am innocent of the blood of all men. For I did not shrink from declaring to you the whole purpose of God."*

Paul did not shrink away from teaching the whole council of God. In doing so he demonstrated profitable ministry to build up the church in the city. He conducted his ministry in public (corporate worship) and house to house (house church or home fellowship), preaching repentance, faith, and most importantly, the Kingdom of God. He recognized his responsibility as a spiritual leader to ensure that clear, sound instruction was given and maintained as a foundation for the work of God.

He also, in concern for the church, commissioned his sons in the Lord, Timothy and Titus, to be an example (I Tim 1:16) of faithfulness to the church and as a part of their duties, set in order the House of God (Titus 1:5) by establishing proper leadership in each church. This remains our pattern.

The premise of this work and the words to follow are this. The house of God, God's intended instrument of revival in the earth, is in need of adjustment. If we are to see the fulfillment of the myriad of prophecies regarding an "end time harvest" it will not occur by wishful thinking or following unwise or unbiblical patterns (often culturally determined). But the house must be put in order. But what is the church to look like? What are the essential, non-negotiables and what are options or preferences that may be permitted, howbeit wise or not. This work attempts to discuss the glorious church Christ died for and continues to build by looking at the scriptures in type, both Old and New. But another word of caution.

On Presumptuous Pontification

In charismatic circles, we have seen the emergence of bishops, now archbishops. I (and we hear of apostles and "arch apostles," whatever they are) can only guess that these honorific titles will eventually lead to cardinals and the Pope of Pentecost! This writer is not a candidate for any of these high titles. My attempt here is sincere, and I will attempt to avoid presumptuous pontifications; merely presenting these musings to stimulate thought and dialog among God's people. If offense occurs, I humbly apologize, as offense is not my intention, but enlightenment is. It seems high time that we take seriously some of these issues, as they are important in fulfilling our high calling in Christ.

"The perfect church service, would be one we were almost unaware of. Our attention would have been on God."

C.S. Lewis

Chapter 2: Four Types of Churches

"Shout for joy, O barren one, you who have borne no child; Break forth into joyful shouting and cry aloud, you who have not travailed; for the sons of the desolate one will be more numerous than the sons of the married woman, Says the Lord. Enlarge the place of your tent; Stretch out the curtains of your dwellings, spare not; Lengthen your cords, and strengthen your pegs. For you will spread abroad to the right and to the left. And your descendants will possess nations, and they will resettle the desolate cities. Fear not, for you will not be put to shame; neither feel humiliated, for you will not be disgraced; but you will forget the shame of your youth, and the reproach of your widowhood you will remember no more." (Isa. 54:1-4)

A few years back I was meditating on Isa. 54:1-4, which lead to a series of messages I preached. In the passage I saw in picture four types of churches which are prevalent today, requiring different solutions. They include:

1. **The Barren Church** – This is a church that has not produced the fruit that God intended for it to produce. Statistics on church growth indicate that the average size full gospel church throughout America is 60 people. The Word of the Lord says we are to shout for joy if we have a small church. Why? Because there is (or should be) anticipation that with God nothing is impossible. With God, even with the worst of situations we can and should bear fruit for the Kingdom of God. That is God's

plan and purpose – not that we should be barren, but we should anticipate and work for the birth of many sons and daughters into the Kingdom of God. Thus, the word to a small church that has either born no fruit or has experienced limited growth should be to get ready to "enlarge your tents stretch out the curtains of your dwellings." That is, stretch your faith to the max. Where it seems like growth is impossible in the natural, God can move supernaturally. That's the kind of church God has called us to be. His intentions, from the beginning, is to see the church of Jesus Christ grow, experiencing multiplication through dynamic church planting until the nations receive the gospel.

2. The second church described here is the **Small-Minded Church** – That is, the church that likes being a small, family church. These churches enjoy the feeling of familiarity; us four and no more. However, by in large God is not into small; God is into large. Everything he did, he did in a big way. From creation to the sending of Jesus as the world's redemption, God did everything well, and with greatness. Every people group, every kindred, tribe, every tongue, and nation; He came to redeem them all. His plan was and is awesome!

But there are many churches that love a nice, intimate family feeling. It's comfortable for them, but it's not God's will for us to be that comfortable. It's God's will for us to be consistently stretching our faith, growing from glory to glory, to greater things all the time. Unfortunately, there are many small-minded people in small, minded churches.

Some of this small mindedness is generational, where there are years and years of the same leadership, not leading, but maintaining status quo. Some have likened them to deacon possessed churches – churches where deacons run everything. A deacon possessed church has leaders who want to do the same things, the way they have always done it. In essence, they tend to be highly religious and mostly sincere people, doing the same thing over and over again out of a sense of obligation or for comfort.

Everyone in a place of service should be looking for a replacement, attempting to find someone to train and equip to take their place. Why? Because once someone is ready to be replaced, God will launch them into a greater arena of service. But if we like the small, comfortable, sweet, and nice, we are never going to fulfill our destiny in God. It is a sad commentary that there remain small, minded people in churches who are fulfilling religious duty, but not fulfilling their destiny. Thus, we must believe that God has a destiny for our respective communities. Each church in a locality is a part of the gateway for salvation and revival in their region or community. Most if not all churches begin small, but with proper Apostolic and Prophetic foundations, they can grow to become godly influences in the communities in which they serve. God is not small minded, and neither should we be.

3. **Shame Based Church** – (verse 4) "Fear not, for you will not be put to shame; neither feel humiliated, for you will not be disgraced; but you will

forget the shame of your youth, and the reproach of your widowhood you will remember no more."

The Western world is filled with people suffering from inappropriate shame. In Western society, over 70 percent of the people have been raised in what's commonly called a dysfunctional family. In spite of this, God still saves us, redeems us, changes us, and if we allow His Word to get into us, will actually renew our minds, so we can live as God intended us to. Our history is not our potential; only God knows all we can become in him.

But there are a great many people who state that they would love to do something for God – if they just didn't have the mother they had – if they weren't saddled with the spouse they have – if they would have had greater opportunities to do this, that, or the other thing. All these excuses, rooted in shame, keep them from fulfilling their destiny in God. The Lord cares less (than we should) about our excuses. Further, many of God's precious children will say things like,

"Well, you know what my temperament is, don't you? I'm a choleric, so I am naturally aggressive, bullheaded, mean, and self-absorbed. Don't blame me, God made me like this."

God has said in his word that he has given us the mind of Christ. We have a new identity; he has adopted us into his family, given us a new name, with a new purpose. His plan is to reorient our lives to his expectations of us, to live up to the name he has given to us. Of course, we cannot do this in our own strength. But He has given us the Holy Spirit, who lives within us and daily helps us. In the midst of our greatest difficulties, we can still live like a Christian, in spite of our background, our temperament, our personality, or any other malady of the past or present. God will empower us. Thus, God does not want us to be the kind of church that is barren, not bearing fruit, or in need of resurrection. Neither does he intend to have small, minded churches, so shame based, or fearful that we stay small for comfort's sake. The church is to be an ever growing, evangelistic organism, reproducing after our kind (the Holy Spirit, not a church label). Thus, He has called us to be the…

4. **Church of the Redeemed** – (verse 5) "For your husband is your Maker, whose name is the Lord of Hosts; your Redeemer is the Holy One of Israel…"

The Lord has redeemed us! A redeemed church has acknowledged who their maker is and are willing to hear his voice and follow his plan until his purposes are fulfilled. That is a church with the same mind as the Redeemer.

What is the mind of Christ for our community? Is it not people saved, discipled, raised up and fulfilling their call in God? His desire is to build a local church to become an influence for godliness in their region. The exact size of the work will depend on many factors, not the least of which include the size of the community, the cultural mix being ministered too, and the giftedness of the leadership. Nevertheless, our heart should be to reproduce, overcome our small mindedness and shame, and boldly face our divine call. To do so, we must recover the missing elements of the church.

"In the Church of Jesus Christ there can and should be no non-theologians."

Karl Barth

Chapter 3: Missing Elements of Church Life

1 Peter 2:1-5 "Therefore, putting aside all malice, all deceit, hypocrisy, envy, and all slander, like newborn babies, long for the pure milk of the word, so that by it you may grow in respect to salvation if you have tasted the kindness of the Lord. And coming to Him as to a living stone which has been rejected by men but is choice and precious in the sight of God, you also, as living stones, are being built up as a spiritual house for a holy priesthood, to offer up spiritual sacrifices acceptable to God through Jesus Christ."

God is building a spiritual house. Though the church meets most often in physical dwellings (a church building, rented hall, homes) it is made up of living stones. Each living stone, a part of a royal priesthood, was brought into the kingdom through the foolishness of preaching and is to be joined together with a corporate body in a given locality. It is God the Holy Spirit that joins us together. It is through his leaders (Five-Fold Ministry, elders, and deacons) that the church is strengthened to maturity and developed for his purposes.

Dr. Paul E. Paino stated, "Great preaching, praying or spirituality alone will not build a great church.

In this chapter we will review some of the missing elements of healthy church life. What keeps churches from growing and becoming everything God intends for them to be?

A church is an organism, it is a living entity, made up of individuals and families from diverse backgrounds, but having a common call and purpose. That common call and purpose is to know God, to follow him, to live according to his plan, to win our neighbors for Christ. The church is all about being a living, vibrant organism. Peter the apostle, in his letter to churches in Asia, describes this organism, and God's intention is to build it.

> *"Therefore, putting aside all malice and all guile and hypocrisy and envy and all slander, like newborn babies, long for the pure milk of the word, that by it you may grow in respect to salvation." (1 Peter 2:1-2)*

Please notice that Peter states that salvation is something that continues to grow. It begins for most of us as an experience – we are saved; but we are also being saved, and we will be saved. It is a continuous relationship with the Lord, characterized by continuous growth. Peter is saying to these born again, spirit filled believers, most likely the leadership of the church.

> *"If you have tasted the kindness of the Lord, and coming to Him, as to a living stone, rejected by men, but choice and precious in the sight of God, you also, as living stones are being built up as a spiritual house for a holy priesthood, to offer up spiritual sacrifices acceptable to God through Jesus Christ," (1 Peter 2:3-4)*

God's plan is to build us up into a fully functional spiritual house, the house of the Lord. As we gather together, whether it be in a warehouse building, in the open air, in a house or a stadium, we are gathering as the house of God. As we come together, we are to lay down our hidden agendas, hurts, anger, jealousy, and petty bickering and rejoice in the awesome presence of God, with intent to learn to love our neighbors as ourselves. As we do so, the church (the house of God) becomes established. As we worship and the Holy Spirit begins to move among us, we are able to lay aside our personal agendas. God's intention for the spiritual house is for it to be so knit together as a living organism that it continues in fellowship throughout the week. The life of Christ in intimate union with each other illuminates our thinking process; for in Him we live and move and have our being (Acts 17:28). Spiritually speaking, we're a house together. Therefore, we are responsible for our place in the house, for our duties to one another. Along with being a spiritual house, we are also a corporate body, requiring leadership and organization for us to work effectively together. Organization or government becomes necessary as we grow in God, as illustrated through the church in Jerusalem (see Acts 2:42-46 and Acts 6).

Getting Organized

Everyone has a place of service. For the church to grow, all of us must find our place and function in it. It took 120 in total unity in the upper room, once filled with the Holy Spirit, to care for the 3,000 souls won to Christ on the first day of the church. God wants unity in the Spirit, in faith, in vision, in purpose so that God can fulfill his purposes through us. It took 120 well trained (by Jesus and his disciples) leaders to properly nurture the new members being added daily to the church. Good preaching is wonderful, but good preaching will not build a church, not by itself. Great praying is important, but it won't build the church. Great spirituality is a blessing, but it won't build the church. To build a great church takes organization or structure. It takes administration, with a plan or a blueprint that everybody understands and is willing to follow for the greater good. The building of a physical house begins in the creative mind of somebody that says, "I have a vision to build a house, a building for a purpose." God is the originator of the vision to build the church. It was his plan from the beginning. With creation, he saw, then he spoke, and it was. He is still the same God, but now he breathes by His Holy Spirit through his leaders, through those who are called into the five-fold ministry (apostles, prophets, evangelists, pastors, and teachers). He breathes through them by the Holy Spirit, giving them a vision to build. Now, what is built may take on differing forms, shapes, sizes, colors, and styles, but leaders are always to build. God gives vision to a man or woman that has been pre-ordained by him. It is a continuous mystery why God gives certain ones visions. God chooses, and whom God chooses he chooses. The vision of God is for both a spiritual house and usually a physical one. God gives a vision, and with that vision he provides a blueprint to follow. The plan is progressive, becoming clearer over time.

The problem with a blueprint is that it takes someone skilled at reading them to know what they mean. In other words, since I am not trained as a builder, I would not fully understand a blueprint if I read it. People tend to see what they want to see, interrupting what they see based upon their perception of truth or reality. In order to understand a blueprint, one must understand or know the mind, heart, and spirit of the one who drew the blueprint, which in this case, of course, is God. Even if a blueprint is understood, the purpose for the drawing will not be actualized without skilled workers, materials, finances, and the rest of the elements necessary to build the house. It's tough to build on a dream alone. It takes tangible material to build a house, whether a spiritual one or natural.

The Need for Structure

"Now at this time while the disciples were increasing in number, a complaint arose on the part of the Hellenistic Jews against the native Hebrews, because their widows were overlooked in the daily serving of food. And the twelve summoned the congregation of the disciples and said, 'It is not desirable for us to neglect the word of God in order to serve tables. But select from among you, brethren, seven men of good reputation, full of the Spirit and of wisdom, whom we may put in charge of this task. But we will devote ourselves to prayer and to the ministry of the word.' And the statement found approval with the whole congregation; and they chose Stephen, a man full of faith and of the Holy Spirit, and Phillp, Prochorus, Nicanor, Timon, Parmenas, and Nicolas, a proselyte from Antioch. And these they brought before the apostles; and after praying, they laid their hands on them. And the word of God kept on spreading; and the number of the disciples continued to increase greatly in Jerusalem, and a great many of the priests were becoming obedient to the faith." (Acts 6:1-7)

Acts Chapter 6 provides a picture of the need for structure. The need for structure was caused by problems in the church.

On the Day of Pentecost Peter preached, resulting in 3,000 souls being saved. A few days later 5,000 more were added to the Kingdom. By the time of this story (Chapter 6) the estimated size of the church is somewhere between 25,000 or 30,000 believers in Jerusalem. By any standard, a substantial church. As of yet, they did not have a building, but met on the back porch of the Temple, called Solomon's Porch. They also met in houses during the week for instruction, to conduct worship, prayer, communion, and fellowship (Acts 2:42-47) together. That was the primary structure of the church. All the work of ministry at the time was done by the apostles and the 120 who were in the upper room. There was no doubt a spirit of unity amongst the 120. They loved each other and worked hard together. As it is with most beginning churches, everyone helped to care for the needs, though in terms of responsibility for planning, direction, and leadership – all was done by the twelve apostles. Up until this passage, in spite of persecution, the church was functioning smoothly. But they ran across a problem that was beyond their time and energy to deal with. The apostles had been focused on laying a solid foundation. The foundation is Jesus. Christ is the Rock we build upon. They were building the foundation on the apostle's doctrine, which was all that Jesus taught to them. The foundation had taken them to this point, but a major problem with the potential of dividing the church emerged.

> *"Now at this time when the disciples were increasing in number, a complaint arose on the part of the Hellenistic Jews against the native Hebrews, because their widows were being overlooked in the daily serving of food. And the twelve summoned the congregation of the disciples and said, 'It is not desirable for us to neglect the word of God in order to serve tables. But select from among you, brethren, seven men of good reputation, full of the Spirit and of wisdom, whom we may put in charge of this task. But we will devote ourselves to prayer, and to*

the ministry of the word.' And the statement found approval from the whole congregation."

The apostles said, 'This is the way it is' and they chose Stephen, a man full of faith and of the Holy Spirit. After choosing him, they commissioned him through the laying on of hands. Please notice a couple of things of importance. First of all, the church had multiplied, yet there was murmuring and complaining. However, in this case it was a legitimate complaint. The apostles did not call fire down from heaven against the murmuring. Instead, they listened intently to the complaints, pursued a course of action filled with wisdom to solve the complaints. Spirit filled leadership, secure in their position in Christ will listen carefully and prayerfully to a legitimate problem and will try to resolve it judiciously. In this case, they found men (it could have been women) filled with the Holy Spirit. All of them were Hellenistic Jews, which is most significant. What always works best is for people with the problem to solve the problem. This shows wise leadership on the part of the apostles.

When someone comes to me with a complaint, I also want to hear two or three suggestions that they have already prayed, and fully thought through that might resolve the problem. If they are looking for me to be the answer, I am going to give them an answer they probably aren't going to like. But when they come with a sincere desire to see a solution, we'll brainstorm together until a plan comes, which will hopefully resolve the problem. It's usually best if those who have the complaint provide the solution for themselves. Find someone among the ranks that is already involved in that area of ministry to solve the problem. Notice also, it wasn't just anybody, these were people filled with the Holy Spirit. They were men of faith (very, very important).

So, they began the process of organizing. Thus, it behooves us to recognize that when the need came, they didn't try and find more apostles to solve the need. That wasn't the first ministry gift that was needed. Pastors were not required at this point. Prophets were not summoned. Evangelists had not been commissioned. Not even elders had been raised up. Deacons, servants, that's what was needed.

There are many churches that have more ministers ("ordained people") than they have deacons or servants. You wonder why things never get done. We don't need more preachers in most local churches. What we need are servants; people that are intelligent enough to see a problem and fix it; and then talk about it later. Not see a problem, talk about it, and do nothing to fix it – which is the typical way that local churches work, unfortunately.

These were men that were chosen because they were already fixing the problem. They had proven themselves faithful and affective ministers as servants of the gospel. So, when it came time for the election, it was very easy to see who should be chosen. These men were already doing the job, so they were the logical choice of the ministry leadership. The decision was not based upon talent or time in the church, but upon faithful service already demonstrated. That's how you chose leaders. It makes no difference if someone has got a title or not. I have visited many churches where 50-60 people are ordained, Reverend this and Reverend that and they rev…but they don't do anything else. I would much rather have people who care less about title and position, and more about work in the

Kingdom of God. We need people who are going to be faithful in the house of God. Summary below:

1. Church multiplied
2. Murmuring (legitimate complaint)
3. Didn't attack – sought solution
4. Found men, filled with Holy Spirit – All Hellenistic Jews (let folks that have the problem, solve the problem)

Another Picture

In this passage, Paul calls for the Elders in Ephesus. Previously, he had instructed Timothy and Titus (no doubt, this was Paul's pattern) to appoint elders within the church. In other words, there was organization wherever Paul went, and he instructed Timothy and Titus to develop accountability systems, howbeit informal no doubt. He always encouraged his leaders, urged them to look for faithful men and faithful women to raise up to take a place of leadership. It was never God's plan to have a one-man band. The Lone Ranger even had Tonto. We were never required to build Christ' church by ourselves. It will not work.

I was listening to David Cho of Korean fame share some of his testimony with a group of pastors in the California area. He was sharing how he had initially built, with great effort, his church to about 2,000. In most eyes, this would be a great work. But he was doing everything himself and was under the impression, according to Korean tradition, that that was exactly what he was supposed to do. He would help lead worship, preach every service, and made sure all the administration was taken care of. He was working 70-

80 hours a week; in fact, he worked himself into a hospital bed.

It was while he was in the hospital bed, near death, that God spoke to him about raising up home fellowship leaders, and the need for prayer. The Lord changed his focus back to the Book of Acts. In fact, Dr. Cho was caught in the cycle of working harder, with limited results, an insidious pattern. Spiritual leaders with much less gifting and cleverness than Cho try; they teach, preach, and counsel, perhaps with hope that other people will be faithful and take leadership. Pastors pour their lives into people, often feeling as though they are taken for granted; sometimes they are their own worse enemy. It's a diabolical problem; it's not of God. Paul recognized the importance of team, of shared leadership to ensure that burnout does not occur, and kingdom work is accomplished. There is a need for structure, and it begins with service; people willing to do work in the house.

Foundation of the Church

When we talk about church growth and development, there are some general statistics to be considered. The average size (numerically) in Western culture is 70 (now a bit less due to COVID) people; a number that has not changed much in 100 years. With Charismatic churches (those that believe in the activation of the gifts of the Holy Spirit) the average is somewhat higher, with the majority of churches settling at 100 or less active members. These churches have been typically called "family churches" and most of them have what they call a "Bell Heifer" in the congregation. Let me explain.

If you have ever been near a cattle ranch, you would notice that the herds have a cow that the rest of the herd seems to follow. The farmer will tie a bell on that cow so he can always tell where the herd is. They call this lead cow the Bell Heifer. There are many churches, family related, that have one heifer in the house, which can be male or female, which everyone tends to follow. Rarely, unfortunately, is it the pastor. But at least the pastor knows how to find the people; they find the Bell Heifer; that's where the people are. The Bell Heifer, usually a long-term member of the church, often a deacon (a deacon possessed church?!) usually likes control and power, though they may do so under the radar. What must be done if a Pastor faces this controlling interest in church? Convert them, chase them, or prepare for Steak! In either case, a church will not likely grow if the Bell Heifer is allowed to lead the herd rather than the anointed spiritual leader appointed by God to lead.

Secondly, there is the "business" oriented church. Usually, this congregation is structured and very task or work oriented, but most of the organization is held in the hands of one or two people. The church grows because it usually has dynamic praise and worship, often with good preaching, and many elements of a larger church, accept it never seems to break beyond the 250 marks. The problem being that since decision making is in a small group of extremely faithful people, new perspectives or insights needed for growth are often missed or ignored. The leaders of the "business church" are often the major givers and workers in the congregation, which is admirable though problematic. It is the typical 20 members of that church doing 80+ percent of the work. Thus, the business church has but a few workers trying to do all the work, with many spectators, sitting in the pews cheering on the works; saying, "Boy, they work hard!" Thus, a key to breaking this pattern is the activation of more workers for the harvest, requiring some to step up, others to step out, all becoming better equipped. More on this later.

The third type of church is the "organizational congregation." These are churches that break beyond the 250-300 level, having upwards of 400-500 adherents. They often plateau, not because of lack of organization, but because they reach the level of gifting of that church. It is usually a strong work. In fact, a congregation with limited debt of 400-500 can do anything their vision compels them to do. In many respects, it is the ideal size congregation. Thus, if they want to do missions, outreach programs or in-house services, they can with limited limitations. Of course, churches this size can become quite content... ultimately, God wants us to continue to grow, and to grow God's way. It is at this point that most churches can begin the planning stage for the planting of daughter congregations, God's preferred method of church growth and Kingdom expansion.[2]

The fourth type of church is the "institutional church," also known as a mega church. I am not talking about a church that has become dead and institutionalized. It means it has an institutional structure, usually consisting of 1,000 adherents or more, with developed departments and leaders over those departments. Each department is self-contained. It's like a church unto itself, related to a much larger work and a much larger vision. Even the budgets of those departments are self-contained. They are able to raise their

---

[2] See Dr. Ken Chants book, **Better Than Revival** by Vision Publishing for more on this perspective.

own support, eventually from their own ministry. I do believe that it is God's plan for churches to be large enough to fulfill God's divine purpose for its existence. Thus, in some cases, it might be judicious for smaller congregations to come under the support and care of a larger congregation (mother church) in order to achieve the greater purposes of God in a locality.

Not every church is designed to be a mega church. Some smaller works are doing exactly as God intended and should not seek to grow beyond their present situation, except as God gives grace. But many are destined to grow, and if your local church has a vision to grow, it must be willing to change. For a church to grow there has to be some changes made. So, let me summarize…

    A. Plateaus (summary above)

        1. 100 or less – Family (Bell Heifer)

        2. 200-300 – Business

        3. 400-500 – Organizational

        4. 500+ - Institutional

Remember, seventy-three percent of full gospel churches are 100 members or less. Sixty-five percent are 60 or less. Eighty-six percent of church growth is transferring growth, i.e., eighty-six percent of local church growth comes from other local churches; that's the present standard. God's plan, of course, is to build a church with new converts, through evangelism, soul winning and discipleship. Soul winning and evangelism means to reach those who have never received and those that are the unchurched that one time believed. Every community has never converted and the burnt stone. The burnt stone believer, at one point confessed Christ, loved God, and many still do (they either watch Christian TV or read the Bible), they pray, often demonstrating a private relationship with the Lord, but they are not in fellowship. Of course, they are out of the will of God. God wants to keep us in the House, actively involved with the body of Christ. There are thousands of people who are no longer in church. We need to reclaim them. We need to have a strategy for their restoration as a part of our growth strategy. We need to also reach those who have never received the Lord Jesus Christ. There are millions of people that have never submitted their lives to the lordship of Christ; to know Christ is to know and have life. It's our responsibility and great honor to reach them with the gospel. Again, let me summarize:

B. Statistics

1. 73% of Full Gospel Churches are 100 or less
2. 65% are 60 or less
3. 86% of church growth is transfer growth
4. Average pastor lasts 3 years

What's wrong with this picture?

In order to change the structure, we need to change or widen the foundation. Congregations must organize and plan for growth. Most churches have various departments, and most have poorly trained leaders responsible for them. Most churches have people who probably could rise to the occasion of leadership but feel ill-equipped to do so. It is not a lack of faith on their part, but an honest assessment.

One of the key responsibilities of leaders (5-Fold Leaders) in the body of Christ is to know those who labor among us, and to equip them to serve in their areas of calling and gifting. Leaders must believe that if and when the message of growth gets into a believer's spirit, they will allow God to open their eyes to see the need for equipping and service. Remember, something had to happen in the disciples for them to be prepared for Pentecost. Thus, as leaders, we must somehow, by grace and with the anointing of the Word of God, get the message into the hearts of God's people that growth is in the heart of the Father, and he wants his children to have ears to hear and eyes to see the harvest that is ripe in the communities where they serve. For the disciples of Jesus day, it required a change, change in strategy, change internally, a breakthrough, or what is called a paradigm shift for the disciples to embrace the Kingdom mandate. We need that too. Churches must shift their thinking away from small and comfortable; to see themselves beyond where they are to the potential they have in the Lord.

Transition

The Lord is preparing his church, putting his house in order. We are in a time of transition…., which requires soul searching for the motivations of the heart, which lead to an evaluation of the foundations of the church and ministry. When done from a biblical perspective, our evaluation should lead to necessary change, a return to biblical patterns, privileges, and purposes of God's word, thus gaining God's perspective, which will likely result in a paradigm transformation leading to growth.

We must remember that great preaching will not, in and of itself produce a great church. Great praying and spiritual exercises alone will not build the church, and thus expand the Kingdom of God. To build the church takes the right materials, the right plan, and the right motivation.

Biblical Reflections

Perhaps some additional brief reflections or pictures from the Word of God can assist our understanding.

The Purpose of God can be found in the beginning. In Genesis 1:26-28 we read:

> *"Then God said, "Let Us make man in Our image, according to Our likeness; and let them rule over the fish of the sea and over the birds of the sky and over the cattle and over all the earth, and over every creeping thing that creeps on the earth." And God created man in His own image, in the image of God He created him; male and female He created them. And God blessed them; and God said to them, "Be fruitful and multiply, and fill the earth, and subdue it; and rule over the fish of the sea and over the birds of the sky, and over every living thing that moves on the earth."*

From the beginning, it has been God's intention to see mankind, under the authority of Christ, to provide government or rulership over the created order. From a general view, mankind is to steward all God has created, according to the truths of God's word. The mandate, to use men and women in equality, motivated from within due to the enduring image and likeness of God within us (now in the Holy Spirit living within us), has never changed. The church needs greater understanding of our mandate, to see

God's Government (see Isaiah 9:6, 11:1-6, Revelation 7:9) manifested in the earth, which is to continue until God's glory covers the earth, and the nations are either discipled or judged. (Habakkuk 2:14, Palms 98:9). From Abraham through the prophets, the intention of God never changed. God still intends to see his Kingdom (government) come in fullness, through His church.

Of course, the Kingdom has come in Christ. Jesus loves and died for the bride of Christ to whom he is espoused. Our focus is to follow the patterns Jesus established in his ministry on earth, and to set in order what remains so the bride can be fully prepared for His purpose.

The Ministry of Christ: Christ is our Supreme Pattern

My premise is straightforward and simple. We need to follow the patterns of Christ to see his purposes fulfilled. Many of God's leaders are seeking strategies to build their church, often borrowed from ministries which have been highly successful. Much of the work done by these successful churches is to the glory of God, and based upon biblical principles, and some of the work is done by clever men and women with extraordinary gifts, sometimes natural and sometimes spiritual. To return to principles and patterns of the ministry of Christ is desperately needed for the church to become healthier and more vibrant. The patterns of Christ himself are key, as is seen in the New Testament.

Jesus called men and women unto Himself- Mark 3:13 reads,

> "And He went up to the mountain and summoned those whom He Himself wanted, and they came to Him."

Jesus called men (and women) to be with him, to see his works and learn his ways. His goal (as seen in the next verse) was to transform them from middle class businessmen (the best potential leaders to work with); then He taught them the ways of God, (see Matthew 5:1,2[3] through modeling the plan of the Father (Luke 4:44, 18,19, John 12:27), with a purpose of preparing a team (Mark 6:7-13, Luke 10:1), who once released under the power of the Holy Spirit would fulfill the purpose of establishing the Kingdom through the church (Matthew 28:16-28, Acts 1:6-8).

Though the disciples were trained under the tutelage of Christ, they did not fully understand the plans and purposes of God, nor did they have power to fulfill the plan of God until after the day of Pentecost, when the church was launched in its fullness. Even so, much of the continuing work of establishing the Kingdom was taken up in the ministry of Paul, who carried the greatest under-standing of the purpose of God to disciple the nations to Christ the King.

---

[3] See Dr. DeKoven's book, What Does God Want: Christian Ethics in the Church.

The People That God Builds With

Several years ago, I had the privilege of pastoring a small but precious flock of people in a local congregation. As a group, none of us were great shakes; not really. I could preach fairly well, and our music was decent; our children's workers cared a lot about children, and our youth did not suffer too greatly under the supervision of the youth leaders.

Sometimes, some new folks would stumble in to visit (not sure how they found us but bless them). Truly, none of us were that gifted, that exciting, that talented…but we loved each other, and shared a common heritage…we were dead, but now we are alive, and a part of the greatest family in the universe. Paul was cognizant of this reality, making it plain as presented to the dynamic church in Ephesus.

Ephesians 2:1-22 reads.

> *"And you were dead in your trespasses and sins, in which you formerly walked according to the course of this world, according to the prince of the power of the air, of the spirit that is now working in the sons of disobedience. Among them we too all formerly lived in the lusts of our flesh, indulging the desires of the flesh and of the mind, and were by nature children of wrath, even as the rest.*
>
> *But God, being rich in mercy, because of His great love with which He loved us, even when we were dead in our transgressions, made us alive together with Christ (by grace you have been saved) and raised us up with Him, and seated us with Him in the heavenly places, in Christ Jesus, in order that in the ages to come He might*

show the surpassing riches of His grace in kindness toward us in Christ Jesus.

For by grace, you have been saved through faith; and that not of yourselves, it is the gift of God; not as a result of works, that no one should boast. For we are His workmanship, created in Christ Jesus for good works, which God prepared beforehand, that we should walk in them.

Therefore remember, that formerly you, the Gentiles in the flesh, who are called 'Uncircumcision' by the so-called 'Circumcision,' which is performed in the flesh by human hands-remember that you were at that time separated from Christ, excluded from the commonwealth of Israel, and stranger to the covenants of promise, having no hope and without God in the world. But now in Christ Jesus you who formerly were far off have been brought near by the blood of Christ. For he Himself is our peace, who made both groups into one, and broke down the barrier of the dividing wall, by abolishing in His flesh the enmity, which is the Law of commandments contained in ordinances, that in Himself He might make the two into one new man, thus establishing peace, and might reconcile them both in one body to God through the cross, by it having put to death the enmity.

AND HE CAME AND PREACHED PEACE TO YOU WHO WERE FAR AWAY, AND PEACE TO THOSE WHO WERE NEAR; for through Him we both have our access in one Spirit to the Father. So, then you are no longer strangers and aliens, but you are fellow citizens with the saints, and are of God's household; having been built upon the foundation of the apostles and prophets, Christ Jesus Himself being the corner stone, in whom the whole building, being fitted together is growing into a holy temple in the Lord; in whom you also are being built together into a dwelling of God in the Spirit."

The Dead now made alive characterizes the people of God. All of us were formerly under the dominion of Satan, caught in lustful lifestyle, by nature children of wrath or in opposition towards God, whether we knew it or not. But thank God, that by His wonderful grace we have been marvelously saved, in order that we might prove God's rich mercy, becoming his workmanship, demonstrating his grace and mercy by our good works as a general part of our lifestyles. As such we must remember that we were once separated from God and his covenant, but now we have become citizens, having become one new man in the earth (the Body of Christ, the Family of God); we are no longer aliens but fellow citizens with the saints from all of history, a part of the Father's household. His ultimate purpose is to fit us all together as a growing, vibrant, and alive holy temple of the Lord, a dwelling place for his Spirit, together fulfilling the kind intentions of his will.

So, what type of people are we to be? Well, first of all, alive is good. That is, people who have been genuinely born again by the Spirit. It saddens me to hear of the many difficulties that have occurred in local assemblies due to leadership that were not regenerated by the blood of Christ. Deacon possessed churches, that is, churches led by (primarily men) insecure people who possess power due to position, but not authority due to their relationship with God. Callings and gifting without authority can destroy the move of God in a region. Alive, born again, Spirit filled, and mature men and women are what the Lord is looking for in building his church, and should be what we are to look for in people we build with.

Secondly, the people that can be worked with are men and women who have become His workmanship... that is, they are actively involved in discipleship with healthy accountability. We all need to learn, grow, and change. Our growth comes through relationship, relationship in the Body of Christ within locality. The best teachers in the world, presented in their writings, through various media will never substitute for local church fellowship, relationship, and accountability. As believers, we are accountable to one another, as citizens of the Kingdom of God. Thus, we are to live in the grace and mercy that we have received, and as the one new man in the earth (Jesus the Second Adam; we are in Him) are to live as ambassadors for Christ, motivated by love, using our gifts and abilities for the glory of God.

A leader will never know the character or motivation of people attracted to a given local assembly. It could be the preacher, worship, etc. God knows what we need, and God knows that with men and women who know who they are in Christ, cooperatively serving as committed citizens with one another and the community they have been placed in, His Kingdom can be expanded for His glory, whether you have great _____ into or not.

"On his robe and on his thigh he has his name written:
KING OF KINGS AND LORD OF LORDS."

Rev. 19:16

Chapter 4: The Heart of a King

For leaders to see the fulfillment of God's purposes, we must have the right heart. The heart of service found in Christ, our King, is demonstrated in his willingness to suffer for us for all mankind. The heart of a King, second to Christ, is though not a perfect analogy, can be seen in the life of King David, as illustrated in 1 Chronicles 28:1-21, 29:1-9 (parts)

> *"Now David assembled at Jerusalem all the officials of Israel, the princes of the tribes, and the commanders of the divisions that served the king, with the officials and the mighty men, even all the valiant men. 2 Then King David rose to his feet and said, "Listen to me, my brethren, and my people; I had intended to build a permanent home for the ark of the covenant of the Lord and for the footstool of our God. So, I had made preparations to build it. 3 But God said to me 'You shall not build a house for My name because you are a man of war and have shed blood.' 4 Yet, the Lord, the God of Israel, chose me from all the house of my father to be king over Israel forever. For He has chosen Judah to be a leader; and in the house of Judah, my father's house, and among the sons of my father He took pleasure in me to make me king over all Israel. 5 And of all my sons...He has chosen my son Solomon to sit on the throne of the kingdom of the Lord over Israel. 6 And he said to me "Your son Solomon is the one who shall build My house and My courts; for I have chosen him to be a son to Me, and I will be a father to him. 7 And I*

will establish his kingdom forever, if he resolutely performs My commandments and My ordinances, as is done now." 8 So now, in the sight of all Israel, the assembly of the Lord, and in the hearing of our God, observe and seek after all the commandments of the Lord your God in order that you may possess the good land and bequeath it to your sons after you forever. 9 As for you, my son Solomon, know the God of your father, and serve Him with a whole heart and a willing mind; for the Lord searches all hearts and understands, every intent of the thoughts. If you seek Him, He will let you find Him; but if you forsake Him, He will reject you forever. 10 Consider now, for the Lord has chosen you to build a house for the sanctuary; be courageous and act. 11 Then David gave to his son Solomon the plan of the porch of the temple, its buildings, its storehouses, its upper rooms, its inner rooms, and the room for the mercy seat; 12 and the plan of all that he has in mind, for the courts of the house of the Lord, and for all the surrounding rooms, for the storehouses of the house of God and for the storehouses of the dedicated things. 13 also for the division of the priests and the Levites and for all the work of the service of the House of the Lord...19 All this, said David, the Lord made me understand in writing by His hand upon me, all the details of this pattern."

29:2 "Now with all my ability I have provided for the house of my God the gold for the things of God...silver for silver, bronze...iron...wood...stones...in abundance. 6 Then the rulers of the fathers' households, and the princes of the tribes of Israel, and the commanders of thousands and of hundreds, with the overseers over the king's work, offered willingly; 8 and whoever possessed precious stones gave...9 Then the people rejoiced because they had offered so willingly, for they made their offering to the Lord with a whole heart, and King David also rejoiced greatly."

In the later years, as in his formative ones, David's heart was filled with godly intentions. His heart, if not his ability, was to build something for the glory of God. Most spiritual leaders can relate to this God motivated desire. He understood, as should we, that God chooses His man, whoever that is. How God chooses remains a bit of a mystery. Most of the great leaders in the Bible were not great in themselves but were made great due to God's endowment (grace). Who God chooses may not be our choice, but apparently he chooses men and or women who desire to provide a rest for God, which is the manifestation of the Kingdom, described in Romans 14:17, as Righteousness, Peace, and Joy in the Holy Spirit.

When the Kingdom is established in the heart of a leader, what will likely be created is a house of honor and prayer, prepared for the glorious presence of God (2 Chronicles 5:11-14), developed from a specific plan, both architectural and operational. God gave to David both plans, and the resources to bring it to pass, even though he was not the man to actually do the building. He made provision for the next generation through his successor, Solomon.

From the principles of this passage of scripture, there are some keys to success for Kingdom builders (Christ, not ours). First and foremost, to David was able to recognize God's voice and his choice (v9), leading to an understanding of the plan (v11-15), both architectural, or the building and the people, and the operational, or how things were to function to bring the glory to God. For the building is not to be haphazard, nor according to someone else's idea, but must be according to a divine plan for a specific ministry. Generally, the plan is…

- Given to leader
- Provided by God
- Not just for the leader but
- For the next generation

Now, let me state categorically, that in the Kingdom of God, one size does not fit all. There are a myriad of ways, strategies, and methodologies which can be used to expand the Kingdom of God through the church. But the leader lacks wisdom who borrows a strategy from another locality or leader, without first insuring that the Lord has indeed determined the appropriateness of that strategy. What works for one leader will not always work for another (in fact, rarely). Each leader must discern, from the Holy Spirit, what strategy is needed to build (living stones primarily, and sometimes physical manifestations, such as buildings) in locality.[4]

In order to see the fulfillment of the plan given by the Lord, God's people will be required to walk in obedience, first to His word, and secondly to the plan given by God, in spite of opposition, which always comes. Thus, it takes courage, for all involved, the courage to act in faith, bolstered by hope, which leads to generous giving of the people, a true

---

[4] For more on how to get a Vision for life and ministry, see *Catch the Vision* by Dr. DeKoven.

sign of revival fires, which releases God's blessing, for the people and the nation(s).

The Operation of a Vision, Begins with the Understanding of the Purpose

As we know from a cursory reading on the life of David, perfection is not required by God for us. David was passionate, passionate for God, passionate for himself. But one thing is clear…David was a man after God's own heart.

David wanted to fulfill the purpose for which he had been created, coming to him via a prophetic word (from Samuel), ordained by God from the foundation of the world.

Well, in similar fashion, every citizen of the Kingdom has been called, saved, placed in His family, to have a vision which will lead to the fulfillment of a grand and glorious purpose. To build, we must know without doubt what the vision and purpose of God is for our lives, our ministries, our communities. Purpose is essential to life. Knowing the purpose to build the Kingdom in locality, requires that we develop goals or objectives, which are clear and measurable. It is amazing to me how many leaders, let alone believers in general, live life without a plan, without goals or objectives. When you develop clear goals and objectives, this gives strength to the plan, which must be specific and clearly communicated, with an intentional feedback mechanism for mid-course correction. It takes leadership with the right heart to see a God sized vision come to pass.

God gave David a plan. It was clear yet required faith and vision beyond himself and his generation. His decision could have been received as pie in the sky by his existing leaders, but David had heard a clear word from the Lord. I am convinced that God intends for churches and its leaders to receive clear vision, dynamic plans, and purposes to build in the natural and spiritual. We must set our hearts to receive the revelation from the Lord and avoid the potential hindrances to the achieving of the plan.

Hindrances to God's Plan

Probably the most powerful and frequent hindrance to the plans and purposes of God being fulfilled in our life is unbelief, a lack of faith in God. Whether through false humility (I don't deserve; really who does?) or fear of success (then I have to be responsible) or failure (I am responsible!) a lack of faith or unbelief is a chief cause of not fulfilling the vision or mission of God.

Second to that is the lack of vision and the ability to plan and follow through. Scripture states that without vision (prophetic insight or revelation) the people perish or will be out of control (Prov. 29:18). A vision or clear mission is essential to the fulfillment of the plans of God, especially as they are related to the growth of the church properly governed.

A third hindrance to the fulfillment of the plans and purposes of God is sin in the camp or the church. This can be a major problem, especially if the sin is primarily in the leadership of the church. Sadly, there has been too much revelation of pastoral and other five-fold ministry misconduct over the past few years, but this should in no wise reflect on the tens of thousands of leaders in the Body of

Christ who live exemplary lives before the church and the world.

A fourth potential hindrance is a lack of understanding of the principles of scripture and how to apply them. Essentially, this is likened to walking in darkness versus light (Eph. 1). A part of the reason for this manuscript is to address this very problem, and to help enlighten the church to the need to set the house in order ourselves, rather than having the Lord do it in acts of judgment.

Fifth, a wrong foundation, such as a denominational pattern or other ministry style, that does not fit the local situation can be a great hindrance to the work of God.

Sixth, if one has poor building material, such as religious people or church transfers who have yet to forgive and grow, this can definitely hinder the work of the Lord. The truth is, as mentioned above, we cannot really choose who we work with. Who we come to the dance with, so to speak, is who we have to dance and go home with. Thus, many times before building, there must be some tearing down of some things, rearranging of others, a ministry of healing and restoration, correction and strengthening, which takes time and patience, but are necessary before building can occur.

Also (seventh for those needing to stay on the count), opposition amongst the leadership can certainly hurt, as can be readily seen in the story of Nehemiah, or for that matter, that of Esther. Opposition from the enemy can be expected but is not nearly as devastating as opposition from "good Christian folks" in the congregation or community.

Eighth, a church or ministry that engages in poor ethics, or wrong business practices, can develop a poor reputation, both in and outside of the church, disqualifying them for ministry, behavior which can hurt the church immensely.

Ninth, any time we launch into ministry, there is a price that must be paid (in time, talent, and treasure). When a church is unwilling to pay the price, whether financially (stingy), or of time it is nearly impossible for the ministry to achieve the purposes of the Lord.

Tenth, and a major problem exported by the West around the globe, is a production versus consumption mentality. That is, when people, from the pulpit to the pew, are more interested in the blessings of the Lord than the Lord and his mission, when the people are motivated to give only to get, when going on a short-term mission is more of a holiday to look at how the rest of the world lives, we are missing the boat entirely.

Finally, simple but profound small mindedness can truly hurt the purposes of the Lord. An example of this became clear when I was teaching on church growth, and one of the saints stated "I don't want to grow. We don't want long hairs, tattooed, pierced sinners in our nice little church." Well, trust me; they would not want to attend that church either. Small minded and closed hearted saints will never help in achieving the purpose of growth in the kingdom of God.

Whatever hindrances there might be, and there are certainly others (pride, etc.), they must be systematically dealt with if growth in the Lord is to progress.

Building According to Pattern
A Spiritual House

In the natural, there are many parts and materials used to build a house. Beginning with the plans, then the foundation, all the way to the roof, building must be done with an end result in mind, with care and excellence. In the Word of God, there are many analogies and illustrations given that allude to building a house, and many words used for parts of a house that have spiritual meanings and applications. Provided here are some of the many scriptures that speak about the need, motivation, process, and materials to build a house pleasing to the Lord.

Deride

Decision to build (Joshua 24:14) "…but as for me and my house, we will serve the Lord." Joshua made the decision to serve the Lord, on behalf of himself and his family. In many cases, God is waiting for us to make a decision in regard to our dwelling. Are we going to dwell in the Lord, with the Lord, under His power, under His anointing? Are we going to be in His house? Are we going to commit ourselves to the house that God has brought us to or not? When will believers recognize that they are in a spiritual gathering by divine appointment (assuming it is a bible believing, worshipping house), for a divine reason?

Whether the congregation you fellowship with is in a little brown church in the vale, a warehouse building, a school, or house God desires for us to fulfill a destiny through the church; but we must make a decision. It does not matter the outward appearance of a facility, or the people attending a congregation, once we have been knit to a congregation we must learn to live in peace and in faithful submission to one another until and only if the Lord sends us to a different place. We must determine that "this is the house that I'm committing myself to."

Joshua had no problem with his commitment. He and his household were going to serve the Lord. What did that mean for him? Well, essentially, whether war (which would come), opposition, good times or bad, it didn't matter, he was fully committed to serve the Lord in the house where the Lord had placed him.

House in Order

It helps to remember that our time on earth is short at best, and the Lord may require you to get your house in order. In 2 Kings 20:1 God said to Hezekiah, "…get your house in order…" Again, no man knows the number of our days, but all things being equal we should live like today is our last, and plan to live to 100 (or more for you special spiritual folks). Of course, when I look back on my earlier years I often say, "You know if I would have known I would live this long, I would have taken better care of myself."

A few years back I was watching a program on C-SPAN. Former Vice-President Dan Quale was featured, from a previous speech he had made on values. One of the things he said was, "It's time for America, it's time for the church, it's time for industry and business to get their house in order." I thought that was pretty significant; even government officials know that we cannot continue with business as usual. The message spoken in America today and being spread around the world is that it is time to change. It is time for the church, especially, to get our house in order. God is requiring of us to make sure we are living right, in our family life, in our church life, etc., as an example to the world of God's intention for the world. We (the church) must get our act together first before we can expect our nations to act according to the dictates of God.

Money's the Answer[5]

Another important point in terms of building can be seen in the story of Nehemiah. In Neh. 12:11, it says that the tithes were restored to build the house of God. We all know that it takes money to build...and God is not poor. Money had been given to Nehemiah to rebuild the walls and to rebuild portions of the City of Jerusalem. In spite of the generosity of the people and the King, there wasn't enough to maintain the house.

God's intention is for the tithes and offerings of the people of God to pay for the house of God. According to the scriptures, the tithes were restored to build the house. If God is really going to build a house, it's going to be done by a joint effort of all the people of God. The average Christian in an evangelical church gives slightly less than 3% of income to the church. No wonder churches and ministries struggle. It was necessary to bring all the tithes into the storehouse, and Nehemiah was not embarrassed to ask for support. Believers should rejoice that we can participate in the life of God here on earth.

Of course, leaders must be generous givers first, thus leading by example. I was talking to the pastor of a local congregation who was trying to determine why their finances were not what they used to be. He had a financial

---

[5] Ecclesiastes 10:19

advisory committee, made up of businessmen in the church that had made a commitment to be a part of giving advice, providing counsel to the pastor on financial matters. Well, naturally his assumption was that his financial committee, at a minimum, was faithful in their tithes and offerings. I asked him, had he checked the giving records? He responded that he felt funny looking at giving. "Well then, I asked, how do you know if they are giving?" Well, it is true that you might never know completely what a person should be giving, but you know if someone is giving $25 a week – they probably aren't tithing, especially if they own their own company. They're tipping God at best!

So again, I asked him to look at the giving records, to see what the problem might be. He found that over half of his spiritual and financial advisors didn't tithe. Each had interesting excuses, "Well my wife doesn't like the church as much as I do. So, she doesn't want me to give. You know we have to be in unity." Another said, "I have been saving it up for a more opportune time to give." Yes, for his Lexus! Wouldn't it be fun if their employer said, "Hey, I would love to pay you, but I'm saving it up and I will give it to you at a more opportune time." You would likely and appropriately say, "I'm out of here!" The fact is, our generosity is a direct reflection of our heart condition, and generous giving is needed to build the house that Christ has established. As leaders, we must learn to challenge God's people to be faithful with their time, talent, and treasure, so the Lord's house can be built for his glory.

House of Prayer

In Isaiah 56:7, paralleled with Matthew 11:17, it says that the house of God is to be a house of prayer. God's intention is for the house, beginning with our own hearts, to be filled with faith filled prayer, praise, worship, and thanksgiving, as a primary focus of our life activities. Often church can be so filled with good activities that we forget the real reason for our gathering, which is to give honor and glory to our King for all he has done.

Unless the Lord Builds the House

Psalms 127:1 says "unless the Lord builds the house, they labor in vain who build it..." As previously mentioned, our goal is not to build a spiritual house, or natural one, in order to fit somebody else's pattern. Few if anyone will ever build another Crystal Cathedral. I admire the architectural marvel built by Robert Schuler and his team. However, I know for certain I could not build such an edifice, nor should I ever consider doing so. This was the vision of Dr. Schuler. Whatever type of house is to be built, if the Lord is not in it, it will never give glory to the Lord. I have seen people worship in warehouses, in tents, in buildings of all shapes and sizes. As long as the building is for the glory of God, and according to the vision of the house, God will be pleased, and the people blessed. As long as the people can gather and worship the Lord, that is the point. But we need to build according to God's plan.

Rock vs. Sand

Matthew 7:24 states that two men were building a house... both in the same area. One chose to build on sand, the other on the bedrock. Of course, the one building on sand was called a fool, and the one building on the rock a wise man. Now who is the rock? Jesus is the rock. Thus, a local congregation must be foundationally built on Christ. As the old hymn says, "On Christ the solid rock we stand."

Most local congregations were founded by a single person or small group, starting out as a Bible study or prayer group seeking the Lord. If the group is of God, it will naturally grow from a small study to a congregation, to a church in the locality with identified leadership. As that work grows, it must continue to build on the rock – solid truth found in the Word of God, not on sand. Everyone who is building their house, their ministry, them self's, their identity on things other than the Word of God, will experience loss when the hard times come. How does one know if a house is built on the Rock? Well, you only really know if it still stands when trouble comes! If a ministry can withstand the trials and troubles of the circumstances of life, it is most likely founded on Christ and his word.

I Will Build (Matthew 16:18)

Matthew 16:18 states

> *"I will build My church, and the gates of Hell shall not prevail against it."*

It is always important to remember whose church we are trying to build. It is not our church, but the Lord's. The church, the ecclesia, was to be a spiritual house, manifested in local congregations everywhere. The ecclesia was made up of citizens in a locality called out to serve or govern in that given area. We are all citizens of heaven, living in the earth, to serve our King. It is his church, we are his people, and all citizens have rights and responsibilities as members of the Kingdom.

Weigh the Cost (Luke 14:28)

Luke 14:28 says that we should weigh the cost before building. Hopefully, a leader or member of a local assembly, is working or serving in a certain place having first because weighed the cost and determined it was worth the effort.

Of course, anytime we make a decision to build, to grow, to change, there will be a cost involved and a lot of hard work to follow. The cost, in dollars, time and energy are rarely known when one first begins, but at least an estimate must be made before beginning a process. Thus, emotion is not what persuades one to build, but logic; simple, profound, well thought out planning.

The Father's House (John 14:2)

Jesus promised that in the Father's house, there were many rooms (John 14:2). His intention was and is to prepare a room in the one and only house that really matters, the Father's house, which has room enough for all... races, nationalities, colors, and gender. There is a place for us in heaven for sure, but between now and then, we need a place to worship here, one that is like the Father's house, with plenty of room and rooms for the whosoever that may come. Heavenly living begins right here. Right here, He is building his Kingdom. He is preparing us now to rule and reign with Him.

Spiritual House (1 Peter 2:5)

We have already covered this, but it deserves mention again. The house we are talking about is first and foremost a spiritual house, made up of living stones, of which we are.

Abraham – City Whose Builder and Maker is God (Heb. 11, Ps. 127:9)

Hebrews talks about Abraham, a man of immense faith who was looking for a city he had never seen before, a city of divine proportions, whose builder and maker was God. Many believe that what he was looking for was heaven, not so in context of Scripture. What he was looking for was the church, for from the beginning of time, God had the church in mind. The church universal, the spiritual building of men and women that would gather together in local settings for the purpose of establishing God's Kingdom is what he was searching for. When we gather in Jesus' name, we are the city which God is building.

"Never, never pin your whole faith on any human being: not if he is the best and wisest in the whole world. There are lots of nice things you can do with sand; but don't try building a house on it."

C.S. Lewis

Chapter 5: The Characteristics of the House

Jesus, quoting Isa. 56:7 stated "My House shall be called a house of prayer for all the nations (Mar. 11:17, Matt 21:13, Lu. 19:46)." That house, as we now know from the New Testament, is a spiritual house, made up of living stones, crying out their praise with joy to our wonderful savior. I especially like how the Isaiah passage reads, beginning in verse 7:

> *"Even those I will bring to My holy mountain and make them joyful in My house of prayer. Their burnt offerings and their sacrifices will be acceptable on My alter; for My house will be called a house of prayer for all the peoples."*

From the beginning, as illustrated in the Trinity, a communion of joy has been the focus and dynamic of prayer, which is a key component of worship (house of prayer would also be the house of worship). As illustrated in the oneness of God (see John 13-17, I am in you, you in me, etc.)[6] there is to be a wonderful dance[7] of joy among all who call themselves children of the Most High God. In many ways, the dance of God that has been from the beginning, was lost in the fall, but all of mankind has been

---

[6] See Dr. DeKoven's *Prelude to a Requiem: Principles of Leadership from the Upper Room,* Vision Publishing.

[7] I am grateful to Dr. Timothy Keller for this concept, found in his outstanding book *"The Reason for God,"* Dutton, NY, NY, 2008.

invited to the dance, provided to us through the grace and mercy of Christ' sacrifice. The dance of intimate, spontaneous, dynamic, and joyful worship is to occur in the House...both spiritual and the natural or physical place where God's people gather to worship the Lord.

Again, as stated above, the word of God provides many examples of the importance of building and building on a strong foundation. Provided here are some samples of principles relating to building from the word. For example, someone had to make a decision to build (Jos. 24:15). Whether the decision was made by direct instructions from the Lord, or due to the sanctified desires (see the life of Paul) of a man or woman of God, someone had to decide... and then get busy. Men such as Hezekiah, who was required of the Lord to get his house in order (which spoke of his own life and the spiritual condition of the nation) did so, bringing deliverance and prosperity to the nation (II Kings 20:1). Further, when the decision was made to build, generous giving of the people was always used to fund the building of the house (Ex. 36:5; 2 Chron 28). The house to be built, whether in the time of Moses, David or in the New Testament, was to be a house of God, which is always a House of Prayer (Isa. 56:7, Matt. 11:17). Though the Tabernacle (of Moses or David) or Temple (of Solomon) were named for their builder (or benefactor), it was always God's house, for his praise and glory.

Of course, we must remember that unless the Lord builds the House, those who labor do so in vain (Ps.127:1). Monuments to men may last for a season, but, as my Sunday school teachers used to say to us children, only what is done for Christ will last.

Whatever is built, whether natural or spiritual, it must be on a solid foundation. The building must be built on solid rock, not shifting sands (Matt: 27:24), for it is not our church, for Jesus said I will build my church, we are his servants (Matt 16: 18) it is a house for his Father (John 14:2), a spiritual House, the one looked for by Abraham, who longed for a city whose builder and maker was God (Heb. 11:10, Ps. 127:9), thus we must weigh the cost before we build (Lu. 14:28), having the right motivation of heart.

Paul makes it clear that the foundation on which the church is built must be strong and sure. Thus, it requires that the church be built on the revelation of Jesus Christ (1 Co. 3:11) and on the ministry gifts of apostle and prophet. That is, the foundation of the church which Jesus builds is based upon the revelation that Jesus is the Messiah, the Anointed One, the Son of God, and very God of very God. Secondly, or in practical terms, the key gifts needed are the gifts of apostle and prophet, which were discussed in the beginning of this work. Solid foundations are essential to a lasting work that will give glory to God and last to the next generation.

Patterns can be found in the Components of a Building

I am not one to search scripture for obscure types and shadows (I leave that for the more intelligent and mystical), but there is often significance to the meaning of words in scripture. Briefly, here are some of the words found in the Bible for the components of a building; they tell us a unique story. Each can add to our understanding of what the Lord wants to build in the House, which He is setting in order. They include:

Temple

In the Old Testament, the temple was a large place, speaking about a place of comfort, growth, healing, rest, or even home. Certainly, it was the one place that King David wanted to be, a place of worship and reflection on the good things of God. The specific words are:

a. Hey Kal- A large building, public place, palace

b. Bayith- Court, daughter, door + dungeon, family, house, palace, temple, prison, and steward.

c. Yasad- Set, sit down together, settle, appoint, take counsel, establish, lay a foundation (which this word speaks of the foundation of the temple), instruct, ordain.

d. Naveh- From H5115; (adjective) *at home*; hence (by implication of satisfaction) *lovely*; also (noun) a *home*, of God, men (residence), flocks (pasture), or wild animals (*den*): - comely, dwelling (place), fold, habitation, pleasant place, sheepcote, stable, tarried.

Temple- New Testament Greek

a. Hieron- entire precinct, central sanctuary, temple, sacred place

b. Naos-to dwell, shrine

c. Oikos- dwelling, family, home, house

d. Theropeia- specifically, healing, but also attendance to medical care within the house or temple.

e. gazophulakion From G1047* and G5438; a *treasure house*, that is, a court in the temple for the collection boxes: - treasury

Royal Priesthood

The temple or tabernacle was the place of worship for the Jewish people. The place where God visited his people. As noted it was a place of healing, family, and rest for all. In Amos 9:11 (also quoted in Acts 15:16), scriptures states it is the booth or tabernacle of David/us Moses and Solomons Temple) that would be rebuilt in the last days (which began in the churches first day, (See Acts 2:17). In Davids tabernacle music flowed, prayer was lifted, all were _____ ... heaven on earth!

* Numbers correspond to Strongs Concordance.

Habitation

Hebrew summary is place of safety, rest, covering for God's people; the specific words include:

a. **gêrûth** *gay-rooth'* From H1481; a (temporary) *residence:* - habitation.

b. z^{e}bûl zebûl *ze-bool', zeb-ool'-* From H2082; a *residence:* - dwell in, dwelling, habitation.

c. **Naah,** nâvâh, naw-vaw'-rest, celebrate, flocks, remain, quiet, dwelling. A primitive root; to *rest* (as at home); causatively (through the implied idea of beauty (compare H5116)), to celebrate (with praises): - keep at home, prepare a habitation.

- d. Maon-Place for God (which is first and foremost our hearts, but also celebrated when we gather for corporate worship) ...
- e. Yashab- set down, dwell, remain, marry, continue, endure, make to keep, tarry
- f. Tiyrah-wall, fortress, castle (place of safety)

New Testament Greek

> Skene skay-nay' – Apparently akin to G4632 and G4639; a tent or cloth hut (literally or figuratively): - habitation tabernacle.

People today are looking for a safe space to live ...peace blessing, prosperity. All of this is provided for in Christ, in who we dwell, and who dwell in us. As we gather, church should be that safe place where mercy and grace are experienced by all.

Tent

> The Hebrew meaning is glory, which is what every true worship center wants, is to experience the wonderful presence of the Lord, guaranteed in the New Testament, as the Lord is with us wherever we go, but especially when we gather in worship together in corporate expression. The specific words are:
>
> 1. Ahal/ohel- covering, clear, shine (as in glory), encouragement (and we surely need encouragement in life), troops, army, battle, drove (warfare)
> 2. Chanah-rest (as to obtain)

To build, in Greek is to edify, prepare, organize building, construction, confirm. The specific words are:

1. episkēnoō, ep-ee-skay-no'-o From G1909 and G4637; to tent upon, that is, (figuratively)

   Abide with: - rest upon.

   a. Sunoikodomeo – construct, company of Christians

   b. Kataskeuazō – to prepare thoroughly, construct, create, build, make, ordain,

   Prepare endomēsis – structure, building.

Each person as to be built u, equipped to serve each other and the world using their talents and gifts for God's glory. Church is to be the place where the encouraging word of God is declared, and his glory revealed.

The components of a house also reveal some of God's intentions for his house. They include:

A. Foundation ...without a firm foundation of strong teaching (doctrine) and a truly personal relationship with the Lord (Spirit) we will not build a strong life or church. Much of this foundation, which is established under apostolic and prophetic government is discussed in Acts 2:42, with my interspersed commentary.

"And they were continually devoting themselves (not occasionally, but continually) to the apostles teaching (doctrine, not doctrines, meaning teaching, based upon a thorough understanding of Old Testament scriptures in light of Christ) and to fellowship (true partnership, committed relationships, deeper than friends, like blood), to the breaking of bread (both intimate meals and the

Eucharist, providing daily or weekly reminder of our relationship with Christ and his body) and to prayer (which probably few of us do enough of, and one would reasonably assume to include praise and worship." These foundations, beginning with teaching the word, are universal.

1. In the Hebrew it is to establish firm, conception or birth, ground firm; the specific word is Yacad-set, sit down together (unity) settle, consult, appoint take counsel, establish, instruct, ordain, set (as in order)

2. Greek is founding, conception, to conceive, the specific word being Themeloo- put down, lay a basis for, erect, consolidate, ground, settle, based upon apostles' doctrine.

B. Walls

1. The Hebrew words provide a picture of protection and inclusion. For certain, many people will visit a church, but not sense the protection of a sheepfold nor the inclusion of family. This is a key to "closing the back door" to visitors and should be a part of our common worship experience. The specific words speaking to this are...

    a. Shuwr/Showr- bull, cow, traveling, walk around (as in prayer?), go sing (As in songs, hymns, and spiritual songs, and making melody in our hearts, Col. 3:16).

    b. Showmah- wall of protection, safety, join (as a place to join together)

  c. Goder-fence, hedge, wall, circumvent

C. Housetop- (worship)

 1. Primarily in Hebrew this speaks of covering.

  a. Oog-roof, top of alter, place of worship

  b. Gaah- (root word) mount up, rise, majestic, glorious, increase, be risen, triumph (which is the goal of our worship, to give the Lord glory, to lift our praise, to "raise the roof" in adoration of our wonderful Lord.

  c. Godiph-tomb, stock of cane, (food, death of self)

D. Windows- Of course to most of us the window provides the opportunity for light to enter a room, often exposing what has been in darkness and transforming the room and everyone in it. Scripture says that the lamp of the body is the eyes (Matt. 6:22, essentially, a window to the soul), making all those who come into the light vulnerable, open to the Holy Spirit, to change or transform, since nothing is hidden from the Lord.

 1. In Hebrew...

  a. Challown-window

  b. Tsohar- light, glisten, make oil, midday or noon, double light (double portion of God's presence?)

  c. Arubbah- chimney, window, (root word) lurk or ambush

      d. Segeph-light, window, gaze, peep, appear, look

E. Doors, which immediately brings to mind Jesus' statement of himself that he was the door to salvation, the Way of entrance (John 10:9). Our worship should always have a focus on Christ, the way maker, who paid the price for our salvation.

    1. Hebrew

        a. Petbach- opening, entrance

        b. Deleth- swinging, gate, leaf, lid door

        c. Mashqouph-lintel, door post (upper section)

        d. Cuph- threshold for bride and bridegroom

    2. Greek Thura- Portal, entrance

The various part of he "house speak to us about what Gods purpose is. Paul stated in 1 Corinthians 3:10 that his assignment, as a foundation building apostle was to be a Master builder (architect). He worked with housetop ministers (pastors, teachers), door openings (Evangelists), window makers (prophets) to build the house God wanted. We still need Master builders today.

Conclusion

We are all part of a building, part of the house that the Lord is building. We must remember that it is God's house, belonging to him, it does not belong to us; we are stewards of all he has created, and are to manage, govern or supervise it for his glory. For it is…

- The House of God - Psalm 127:7
- Which belongs to Christ, thus… - Matthew 16:18
- We must make a decision to build, It is… - Joshua 24:14
- A house of prayer, built - Isaiah 56:7, Matthew 11:7
- On the rock, which is Christ - Matthew 7:24
- Thus, we must weigh the cost - Luke 14:28
- With generous giving - Nehemiah 13:11
- Because it is the Father's house, - John 14:2
- A spiritual house, and we build… - 1 Peter 2:5

Until we find that city whose builder and maker is God.

Some Final Thoughts

We know that Jesus is still building His church, via the proclamation of the Kingdom of God. His Kingdom is here, now, but not known by normal observation; it is in the

Spirit. A natural outgrowth of the proclaiming of the Kingdom of God is the conversion of new souls, and the expansion of God's wondrous Kingdom through planting churches everywhere. These churches, if planted and nurtured with principles of life and truth from the word of God, will no doubt continue to reproduce, and the cycle will continue, forever. Of course, our motivation to evangelize and plant is rooted in the marvelous grace and mercy (Agape) of God; it is all about Him, for Him and through Him. Our continued work, which should always flow from the easy yoke of the finished work of Christ on the cross as we expound the Great Commission program of making disciples of all people groups, motivated by the Great Commandment to love our neighbor as, or greater, than ourselves.

Thus, in spite the dysfunction often seen in modern church life, form mega church madness to House church hide and go seek, and all points in between, thank God His church is alive and will continue to thrive, ever-growing and maturing, and will fulfill its God-intended destiny of filling the earth with the knowledge of the glory of the Lord as the waters cover the sea.

Other Books by the Author

Assessment in Counseling

Christian Education

Crisis Counseling

Family Violence

40 Days to the Promise

Fresh Manna

From A Father's Heart

Grief Relief

Healing Community

Homiletics

I Want to be Like You Dad

Journey Through the New Testament

Journey Through the Old Testament

Journey to Wholeness

Living Fruitfully

Marriage and Family Life

New Beginnings

On Belay!

Parenting on Purpose

Pastoral Ministry

Prelude to a Requiem

Research Writing Made Easy

Strategic Church Administration

Supernatural Architecture

That's the Kingdom of God

Transferring the Vision

Twelve Steps to Wholeness

Visionary Leadership

www.ingramcontent.com/pod-product-compliance
Lightning Source LLC
Chambersburg PA
CBHW071159090426
42736CB00012B/2387